READ THIS WAY

STOP!

You may be reading the wrong way!

In keeping with the original Japanese comic format, this book reads from right to left—so action, sound effects and word balloons are completely reversed to preserve the orientation of the original artwork.

Check out the diagram shown here to get the hang of things, and then turn to the other side of the book to get started!

CONTENTS 9

Chapter 66: Like-Minded

Rrooohh!!

It's so bright!!

Wh-What's that light...?!

Huh?!

BSHAA

Nothing's happening to us...

What a warm, gentle light...

They're all vanishing!!!

It's just the shades!!

The shades...?!!

BSHAA

BSHAA

BSHAA

BSHAA

BSHAA

BSHAA

You will
never come
near Fairy
Tail again.

From now on, you will have to worry about your safety constantly.

Both of us will.

Now that you're a bungler of such epic proportions, the Council can't overlook your actions anymore.

KAK

KAK

KAK

SWOOOOO

KAK

KAK

Now he's mine!!!!

It's just like the last time!!! He doesn't even see me coming!!!

Your dragon-slaying magic...

Where... did you learn it...?

SHOP ROLL

GRRR

Shut your hole...

You can tell me that at least, right?

Hey! This is the first time I've ever met anybody who uses the same magic as me!!!

So you *were* taught by a dragon after all!

SHF !!

SHF !!

The Steel Dragon, Metalicana.

!

Metalicana.

Who knows?

What happened to the dragon?

You too?

Oww...

Ouch...

And I told you that I don't know, you trash!!!

I · asked · you · what · happened?!!!

GONK

It disappeared on me!!

?!!

What did you say?!!

Just talking to you makes me feel like my brains have burned to ash!!

One day, Metalicana just wasn't there anymore!

Gone, without even saying a word!

!!!!

Are you saying that you know where Metalicana is?

Don't be stupid!!! The one I'm looking for is Igneel, the Fire Dragon!!!

!!!!

H-Hey...

That wouldn't be seven years ago on the seventh day of the seventh month, would it?

Dammit!! That stupid, selfish...

14

Seven years ago... Year 777, on the seventh day of the seventh month... two dragons vanished?

Why does it have all those sevens in a row?

How should I know?!!

This is our guild!!! You're the one who should go!!!

If you're going, then hurry up and get gone.

Humph... Well, it makes no difference to me.

SHK

We're both dragon slayers, right?

Why should I?!! Don't give me that crap!!!

If you learn anything about Igneel, tell me, okay?

So wash your neck and get ready for Gajeel's axe!!!!

The next time we meet, you're dead!!! Got that?!!!

You're unhinged, huh?

Now that we're even, I thought we'd make nice a little.

That does it!! I'm not going to be nice to you now!!!

It was you guys who messed up our guild, right?!!

Just who's unhinged here?!! Look what you did to my guild!!!

Well, this time...

...we sure made a mess, hm?

That's some face you have on there.

Hmm?

Master ...?

U-Um...

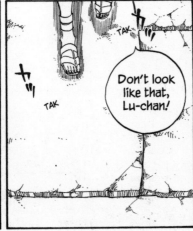

TAK

TAK

Don't look like that, Lu-chan!

...it can always be built up again!

Sure, it left the guild in ruins, but...

Not after everybody pitched in and won this fight!

Oui!

Sorry to make you worry about us, Lu-chan!

Levy-chan...

Jet... Droy...

Reedus...

I heard all about it. Not a person here blames any of this on you.

No...

This is all my...

Lucy.

I...couldn't help... I, um...um... I'm sorry...

...but we can share them to a certain extent.

We can't share in them completely...

Happiness... ...and sadness...

One person's anger becomes everyone's anger.

One person's happiness is everybody's happiness.

That's what a guild is all about!

And one person's tears are everyone's tears.

So lift your head up.

You should already know how everybody feels.

There's no need for you to feel guilt.

You are a member of Fairy Tail after all.

HIC

PLIP

PLIP

SNIFF

HIC

WAAAAAH! WAAAAAH! WAAAAAH! WAAAAAH!

WAAAH! WAAAH!

WAAAAAH!

This is going to bring the wrath of the Council down on us... Hey, if we handle this badly, we could even end up in jail...!!!

SHUDDER

SHUDDER

But even so, they really did make a mess here.

22

Chapter 67: My Decision

It had been a week since the battle with Phantom.

And we'd finally found a bit of calm to start heading forward...

KANG トン

KANG トン

TENK テン

TENK テンヤン

DONK

カン

DONK

...but just after that, something terrible happened.

SHNK

SHNK

SHNK

SHNK

We were suddenly completely surrounded by the Council's soldiers, the Rune Knights.

We are the Rune Knights, enforcement and detainment division, under orders from the Magic Council!!!

Nobody move!!!

Master! Pull yourself together!!

WAAAH!

Don't even try, Natsu. They'll catch you anyway.

EVERYBODY, RUN!!!

So they sniffed us out already?!!

Aw, man!

The Rune Knights "requested and required" us to accompany them to their base camp for an extended investigation.

Fairy Tail's disposition would be taken up by the Council and decided at a later date.

After an entire week, things finally settled down.

We underwent questioning every day.

:
Sigh.

All the evidence and witness reports indicate Phantom instigated the attack.

SKRCH SKRCH SKRCH SKRCH SKRCH

But you don't need to worry, Mama.

I doubt they can judge us too harshly.

It's...just a bruise. It won't be there permanently, right?

CHIK

Oww...

CHEEP

CHEEP

Say, Mama... Was this whole thing really being manipulated behind the scenes by him?

I know how he is, but I didn't think that even he would go this far...

Phantom, huh...?

I'm working! Leave me be!

Um...

Hey, Papa! I made you a rice ball!

TAH

DAH

Yes, sir...

Say...

Can't you understand when I tell you you're in the way, Lucy?!!!

34

Then you don't mind if I have it?

Go right ahead!

TREMBLE *TREMBLE*

Don't be ridiculous! I can't eat something when I don't even know where it came from!!

GONNNG

Hm?

ZOOM

Juvia got up so early just to make it.

SLUMP

Juvia is sorrowful!!!

Okay, I'm digging in!!!

H-Here... Could you give them to Lucy?

WOBBLE

Keys?

Lucy's keys?

JANNG

Natsu, Gray...

!

:

Mmm!!! This is really good!!!

A-Anyway, how's Lucy... doing...?

Mmm!!

If you had just said something, we would have helped you.

No, I...Ha ha ha...That's what I get for being a feminist.

You...You don't look so good. I haven't seen you in a while. You were looking for these all this time?

Yeah, maybe... I'm a little worried...

Why don't we drop by and pay her a visit?

Aye!!!

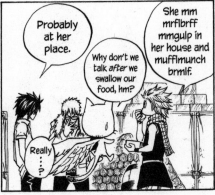

Probably at her place.

Why don't we talk *after* we swallow our food, hm?

She mm mrflbrff mmgulp in her house and mufflmunch brmlf.

Really...!?

?

Yeah, well that was then, and Lucy is Lucy, you know. Oh, well.

No...I think I'll pass. You know, right? I've got some bad memories about celestial wizards...

Loke, you've never been to Lucy's place before, huh?

36

Huh? She isn't here!

I admit a bit of anxiety myself.

After screaming at us so much, you came along?

......

It looks like she's not home.

You even checked her bath?!!

She isn't in there, either!

Maybe she's in the bath!!! I know I promised not to do this. But what with the circumstances, I think you can forgive me for—

Why else? She's a runaway, of course!!

Then why'd she write them in the first place?

I wonder why she never mailed them?

They're all letters to her mother?

To Mama...

To Mama...

What do you think, Erza?

I'm going home

Lucy left a note.

What's wrong?

Hm?

40

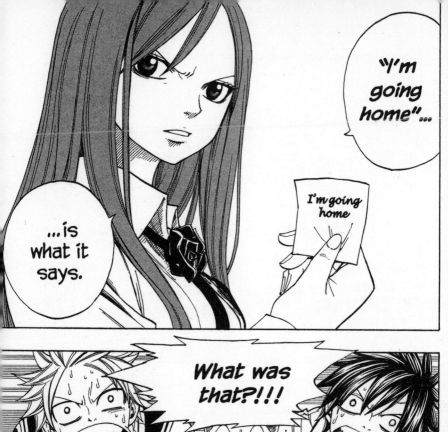

"I'm going home"...

...is what it says.

I'm going home

What was that?!!!

Let's go find Lucy's family!!!

I don't know!! Anyway, let's go after her now!!!

Sh-She wouldn't be doing this because she feels responsible, would she?

What does she think she's doing?!!

"Going home?!!" What's that supposed to mean?!!

Chapter 68: Goodbye

The
Heartfilia
Estate

It's the
young
mistress
!!!

It...
It...
It...
It...

Waaaaaah!!!

The young mistress has come home!!!

CHATTER

It's the young mistress!!!

What was that you said?!!

BWOHHHH

WHAAAAAHH

Spetto-san, I'm sorry to have worried you so much.

SNIFF SNIFF

Young Mistress...I'm so happy to see you safe... I-I can't believe that you're really back...

MURMUR

Lucy-sama!!

Welcome home!!

It's been a whole year!! Where have you been?!

Young Mistress!!

MURMUR

You haven't been avoiding your magical sciences lessons, have you? Remember that celestial wizardry is dependant on trust and love... mumble mumble...

Some new books have come in from the East.

Yes! I'm just fine on that account!

Lucy-chama? Haven't you kept up with magic sciences?

MUMBLE
MUMBLE

I wasn't eloping!

Well?

ZNORF

The young mistress is the right age! Did you run off with a man a time or two?

You young people these days are always...

There's no law against eloping, Young Mistress!!

Bero, old boy! That's enough of that question!! Besides, the young mistress is in this direction!!

Lucy-chama, have you kept up with—

ZNORF

Ah ha ha ha!!

"Booo?"

BOOOOOOO

I just... I just... !!!!

His runaway daughter has come back, but he sends a servant to summon me to wherever he is at the moment.

SIGH

He hasn't changed a bit!

!

Young Mistress!! The Master requests your presence in the main house study!

CHATTER

They haven't changed a bit...

CHATTER

It's about time you were back.

Lucy!!

I deeply regret my actions in that regard.

I humbly apologize for leaving the house without making my intentions known.

...I was on the verge of using my money and influence to see that guild crushed.

You made a wise decision coming back. If you had stayed at that guild any longer...

I assume you will take this as a lesson about how your willful actions can bring trouble to those around you.

So you've finally grown up, have you, Lucy?

There is only one reason I have brought you back here.

Your wedding arrangements have been made.

That makes you different from other people. You live in a different world.

You are the daughter of the Heartfilia family.

I hear he said to you that he's had his eye on you.

Duke Sawarr, son and heir to the Junelle family.

Lucy-sama! ♥

Yahoo! ♥

He said something like that.

With your marriage into the Junelle family, Heartfilia Railways will receive the land it needs to continue its southward progression.

Your wedding means a vital part of securing our future.

That son will inherit the Heartfilia estate.

Of course, you will be expected to bear a son.

That concludes our discussion.

Father
...

You may now return to your room.

!!!

I think you've completely misread the situation!

The only reason I came back was to let you know my decision.

I actually do feel that leaving without notice was a mistake. It was nothing more than running away.

So this time, I am going to tell you exactly how I feel!

I am leaving this house !!

I don't need money or fancy clothing!!!

What I need is a place where people accept me as I am!!!!

And it is so much better than my first one!!!

Fairy Tail is a second family for me.

I've been away only a short time, but it's been very hard for me to live apart from the house in which Mama lived.

Spetto, Old Man Bero, Ribbon, Aed...

It was, and is, very difficult to part with them all.

!!!

AAAAH!!

But if Mama were alive today...

...I think she would have told me to do what I feel is right!!

To Mama in Heaven...

This town you come from is pretty big!

You know, I...

Ah...No! This is just the garden. Everything from here to beyond that mountain is my family's place.

After all, Fairy Tail is a part of me now.

Such a blue sky...

Oh no!! Commander Erza is broken, too!!!

Natsu and Gray have gone bye-bye. Commander Erza, could you say a word, please?

And she brags with such a casual look on her face!

The young mistress has arrived!!

Huh? What's with you guys?

...I don't think I could keep going without everybody's help.

FAIRY TAIL

FAIRY TAIL

Name: Laxus Drayer Age: 23 yrs.

Magic: All Forms of Lighting Magic

Likes: The Powerful Dislikes: The Weak

Remarks

One of the most powerful wizards at Fairy Tail. He is really bad at interpersonal communication, so he is commonly found alone. The things attached to his ears are headphones for the magic sound player, Sound Pod. His favorite music genres are classical and rock.

Chapter 69: Next Generation

What?! Me?! Perish the thought!!!

Fwa ha ha ha!!!

!!!

You didn't fall asleep, did you?

We are in the middle of a trial...

HEH

But for Fairy Tail to be judged completely *innocent* was a true accomplishment!

Well, the disbandment of Phantom Lord...

...and the forfeiture of Jose's title of wizard saint...

...were all things I expected to happen.

It was all thanks to my defense!!

You'd better thank me, Mabô!!

Magic Council Member

Sixth Seat, Yajima

Once we've got the guild rebuilt, come by for a drink!

And the ramen's on me!!

I'm in your debt, Yanbô!

Oh, all right!!!! Have twenty slices, thirty slices, whatever you want!!!

May I remind you that violence between guilds is a direct violation of the fourth clause of your guild charter?

A dozen slices is just right.

A dozen slices is too much!

Fairy Ramen! And don't forget the dozen slices of *chashu* pork!

Ahh...So you've fallen under Loke's magic spell too, huh?

By the way, I don't see Loke.

No, I haven't!!!

CLAMOR

CLAMOR

Ah ha ha!!

What's all this? Normally they just laze around and drink up all the liquor!

CLAMOR CLAMOR

But you lost your keys. Weren't the spirits upset at you?

Okay. If I see him, I'll be sure to mention it.

Ha ha...

I just wanted to say a word of thanks...

But...I hear he found my keys for me...

CHANK

Oh, dear...

Just remembering makes my rear end throb in pain...

SLUMP

Didn't I?!!!

I told you never to drop my key again, little girl!!!

AAAAAH!!!

Yeah, well... the word "upset" might not be enough...

69

Are you a demon or something?!!!

If we gave it a stinging burn, I wonder what kind of face Lucy would make?

GWOOOGGH

I don't want outright harassment either!!

Lucy, show me your red, shiny butt!!

FWAFF FWAFF

Please spare me your casual sexual harassment.

I could ice it down for you.

SHINNG

!!!

GA

GOWHAM

CHATTER

CHATTER

Just you try to say that one more time!!!!

Erza?

CHATTER   CHATTER

Let me spell it out so you really understand!!!

This guild has no need of weaklings!!!

I can hardly show my face anymore out of shame!!!

Those wimps from Phantom were able to show us up!!!

You cretin...

I'm talking about you!! And you!!

That S-class wizard, Laxus?

That creep! Coming back and mouthing off.

Laxus... So he's back?

AH HA HA HA HA HA

You guys are pathetic!!!

This all got started when you got your butts handed to you by Gajeel, right?

How dare you...

You know, I don't even know your names!! Who are you?

Laxus!!!

Well, well!! If it isn't the chickie who's the root cause of it all!!

How many people have come after you for not taking part?!

Nobody!! And that's because the Master left orders not to!!

It's all over now!!

And from the start, nobody here was ever interested in playing the blame game!!

Is that a surprise? That fight had nothing to do with me!!

Still... If I had been here, we'd have never been brought down like that!!

Ah ha ha ha!! What kind of fight would it be when you can't even touch me?!!

Laxus!!! Come on and fight me, you heartless creep!!!!

Wha?

When I inherit the guild, I'm going to clean out all of the weaklings!!!!

The weaklings and anybody who tries to oppose me—every last one!!!!

It'll be the most powerful in history, and nobody will ever think of giving us any crap!!!!

This guild will be the strongest guild there is!!!!

They may not be empty...

?

"Inherit?" Listen to the man make empty threats!!

あはははは!!!
AH HA HA HA HA HA!!!

GRUNCH!!

GRUNCH!!

Laxus is the Master's grandson.

Whaaat ?!!!

But...I'm against that!!

I would never want a master who feels that way about his fellow guild members.

Y-You're kidding...

So when the Master retires, the odds that Laxus will become the new Master are extremely good.

They're just rumors. In reality, nobody's ever heard the Master mention anything about who the next Master will be.

You mean he's waiting for that creep to shape up?

It's for that reason the rumors about the Master being unable to retire are flying around.

It's over. If we expend our energy on him, we'll just exhaust ourselves.

That jerk...

Do you feel like taking on a job?

Let's turn to a more pressing matter. What do you think?

WHOOOOOOOOO

おおおおおおおおっ

You guys are huge!!!

Th-That's true, huh...?

Well, if she brought out Aquarius, I doubt I could win against that.

Um, Lucy?? On the greatest team??

I like it!!!

The official formation of Fairy Tail's greatest team!!!

Very well. Here's our first job!!! We're to go and take down a secret magic fraternity in the castle town of Lupinus!!!

SUBDUE

500000 J

FLIP

Any complaints?

No!!! We're overjoyed!!!

Y-You mean with him...?

Yeaaah !!!

Let's go!!

THUNK

Ahhh!

GLUG

GLUG

We're renovating the guild...

Maybe it's time for a new master too...

Retirement, huh...?

And Mysto-gan...

He's the poster child for "uncom-municative"...

Gildarts is out of the question...

Laxus...

He's got a big attitude problem.

She's so young, but... Erza...

So the only one left...

It looks like they're at it again!

Huh?

Hm?

Master, so that's where you were...?

Apparently Erza's team took a job and destroyed half of the town again!!

!!!!

OHHHHH

Huh? Master? What's the matter?

The Magic Council wants a written letter of apology immediately!

TWIK

Who can retire like this?!!

Chapter 70: Frederick & Yanderica

SIGH...

HAHH

SLUMP

Hm? What's got you so down in the dumps, Lucy?

I'm out of money...

SNIFF

We go out on high-paying jobs, but Natsu and Gray tear the towns apart, so we end up giving most of it back in reparations.

I'm not rich!!! I never received even a tiny bit of money from my family!!!

That's not what I'd expect to hear from a rich girl.

WOOSH

TONK TONK

This sport takes too much skill for you!

All right!! I go first!!

I'm all worried, and look at them!

Where did you guys get that thing?!

コツォォォ

KRAK

GWOOGH

GRUNCH

GANCH

Hyaaahh!!!!

That isn't how the game is played!!!!

Don't be ridiculous!!! It's five!!! This one is only cracked!!!

That's our Natsu!!

Tsk! Six, huh?

ふしゅうぅ
PSSHHHH

Waaaah!! If it keeps up like this, I won't even have enough to make this month's rent!!

I don't think that's actually true...

As you can see, they're only happy when they're breaking things.

I think it's right up your alley, and you don't have to worry about anything getting destroyed. ♡

Then how about I recommend a job for you?

Hm?

A large town with far more business opportunities than Magnolia.

And so I arrived in the town of Onibas.

So we're supposed to use our magic to help an unpopular theater draw in customers again, huh?

Natsu, we're here! Pull yourself together!

I will never board a train again... Urk...

SLUMP

I don't think we're supposed to be *acting* in the plays.

Ahhhhhh!

Ahhhhh!

Ahhhhhh!

Voice training?!!

AHEM

How-ever...

It sounds like fun, doesn't it? ♡

Yeah, this isn't a bad time to study theater from behind the scenes!!

And when I get my novel finished, I want to turn it into a play!!

Hmm?

APPLE

APPLE

Let's give them the best show we can! ♡

Our job is nothing more than staging.

For example, Natsu will make fire. I'll try to sing some lyre-based songs to create the right mood.

BOOK STORE

Whoa!

Isn't it a nice-looking place?

Thank you very much for taking on this assignment.

Um...Are you the folks from Fairy Tail?

Scheherazade Theater Company
Presiding Director, Rabian

POIT

About that... I've run into a bit of a problem...

?

Yeah!! We're here to help with the staging! Leave everything to us!!

Whaa?!! All of your actors have run out on you?!!

Yes, thank you very much.

Thanks for what?!!

The reputation of our public performances has gotten worse and worse!

As time went on, the actors became too embarrassed to even appear in my plays.

And although I'm glad you came here, I'm afraid there is no play to put on, thank you very much.

I was wondering what the story would be.

Heh!

I think you need to learn the rules for thanking people.

This is the only way of life left to me!!! Thank you very much!!!

Thirty years ago, I quit my job, and started down this path.

As a result of my chasing my dream, my wife stopped loving me and left.

Sh-She's glowing!!!

Ehh?!!

GLEAM GLEAM GLEAM

But if you need actors, they're standing right in front of you!!

I was correct to work on my voice training.

I never knew you wanted to act that much!!

PLIP

We don't want to see a man's dream end like this!!

I'm almost certain those parts won't be in the play.

I can play the entire range of characters from fire-breathing vegetables to fire-breathing fruit!!! But which to play?!!

S-Sure... It sounds like fun ...

You mean, you all...

But you know, your script is really terrible.

Yes, thank you very much.

That would have been a good time for a thank-you.

Well, maybe I'll let you give it a try, huh...?

Tsk! Amateurs...

rock

Everybody really got into it, and had lots of fun!

...and spreading promotional leaflets.

We were busy with rehearsals...

Only a week to go before the opening.

21
AUGUST

And on opening day...

Oooh!! This is the first time I've seen this big an audience, thank you very much!!

CHATTER
CHATTER
CHATTER
CHATTER
CHATTER

OOOOH

オオオッ

Wow!!

What just happened?!!

You will eat my sword of ice!!!

Gwaah!!!

I don't know what happened, but he's kind of weak, huh?

OOOOOOH

Th-Th-That is...nothing!! I have...ten swords to my...name!!

Don't you think that's rushing things a bit, Frederick?!!!

P-Princess Y-Yanderica... we must... make lots of...children!!

Frederick-sama, how can I ever thank you?!

But you're the one who called the darned thing!!!! What kind of plot twist is that?!!!

Y-Y-Yes... that is what I wish too!!

Now that it's come to this, we must team up to defeat it!!!

And the guys just run away?!!!

Th-Thanks, Princess!! I owe you one!!

Right!!

You two, run like your tails are on fire!!

TMP TMP TMP TMP TMP

Hey, what do you think you're saying, Princess?!!

I will stop the dragon!!

Ah!!

Gah?!!

This huge costume is...really heavy...

Hey...Don't you think this play has gone overboard...?

CHATTER

CHATTER

This play is beyond the pale...

!!!

GRUNNCH

Kyaaaa
!!!

OOOGH

FWOOGH

GONK

BWAAG
!!

Right!!
Ice
make—

!

Gray,
help
me!!!
Ice!!!
Ice!!!

EYAAAAA!!!!

ZLISS ZLISS ZLISS ZLISS ZLISS

You're not only a bad actor, but you took the part way too far!!!

Princess... A-A-Are you all... right?

SST

HWEET-WHOO

That's great, Princess!!

GWAA-

-AAHH

That hurt!!!!

CRASSSHH

KRIK

KRIK

KRIK

I knew it!!!!

HA HA HA

HA

HA

AH

Bravo !!

Ah ha ha!!!

Now that was something to see!!

DWOOO

!

That was great!!!

あっはっはっはっは

CLOSED

That was wonderful !!!

SOLD OUT

Frederick & Yandérica

You guys are pretty good for hammy actors!!

Gah ha ha ha!!! I never imagined this would be such a hit!!

POIT

Ahhhhh!! Ahhhhh!! Ahhhhh!!

Your attitude is a complete reversal from when we met you...

Three performances a day is overkill!!

Hey! Will you just pay us our reward money now?!!

Don't just sit there!!! We have a performance to prepare for!! The curtain goes up again today!!!

I want to go home!!!

FAIRY TAIL

Chapter 71: A Night in Impatiens

TWITCH

Lucy !!!

Oh, this is perfect!!! When you returned my keys—

You guys are too?

You're on a job in this area too?

Well, this is a coincidence!

ZINNG

Well, I have work to do, so...

ZOOOM

This is a village just a little to the west of Magnolia.

Impatiens Village.

It's a tourist village made up of Oriental-style buildings.

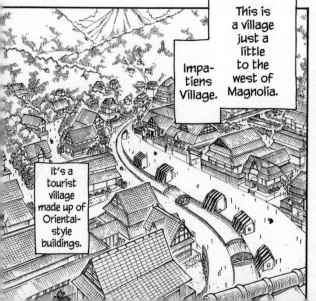

Did you do something awful to him? I'm pretty sure it's you he's avoiding.

What was that supposed to be?!

I haven't done a thing!!

Our job this time was to take out a bandit gang that was holed up in the ruins of a nearby fortress.

We finished the job earlier than expected, so we decided to stay over an extra night.

What's the problem with that jerk Loke?!

Human?!!
And...And you
can talk?!!

Aye!

Aye?

Huuh
?!!!

Tsk! I calculated
that I could keep you
fooled for a week
considering how
dense you are, Lucy!

Such
generous
calculations.

Yes, yes. You can
stop the stupid
tricks and come
out now.

I am the
servant of the
hero who bears
the sacred
stone. Puun.

HEH
HEH

!

Hi,
pretty
girl!

By the way,
where are
you going?

With those
guys having a
pillow fight, I
could get hurt.
So I thought I'd
go for a walk.

We're here from Oshibana.

What do you say? Want to come have a drink with us? It'll be funky!!

SHF SHF SHF SHF SHF SHF

That kimono looks nice on you.

Are you a tourist?

Aw! Don't be that way! We won't keep you long!

Nope. Sorry.

SHF SHF SHF SHF SHF SHF SHF TAK TAK

Sorry, but I'm not alone.

! ! ! ! ! ! ! !

SHF SHF SHF

Puuun!

TRMBL TRMBL TRMBL

! ! ! !

When you say you're not alone. Do you mean you're with that cat and...

Happy!! Do something!!

Come on!!

S-Sure... You've got some funky friends! They can come too!

Back off, guys!

She talks to her cat! How cute!!

What do you mean, "Nyaa!?"

Nyaa!!

Heh heh heh!

It's not like that!!!

These guys are wizards?!!

This could be bad...

We'll have a funky good time!!

Let's go and have a good time!!

Huh...?!! What's going on...?

My body isn't moving...!!!

Listen guys!! Will you cut this out—

EBB AND SEA BREAM

MIND | SKILL | BODY

．．．．．．

I've been wanting to ask you this for a while, but...

...did a celestial spirit wizard do something awful to you?

S-Sorry...!

Ha ha...

YEAH! YEAH!

Say...Why are you sitting so far away...?

Sorry. Really... If I hurt you, I apologize.

Why're you talking like we're a couple about to break up?!

I'd rather you just forgot about me.

If you don't want to talk about it, that's okay with me, but just to let you know, I'm not that person.

Yeah... I know.

GRR

GUM

MPH

!!!

Wh- What ?!

GWMM

Y- Yes?

Lucy...

FAIRY TAIL

6B-11

Chapter 72: The Star That Will Never Return to the Sky

124

Did that draw you in?

That's one of my best pick-up lines!

It gets them all emotional, don't you think?

Well? Didn't it work on you a little?

. . . .

SLAP

YUP, YUP.

VWAA

...I really hate jokes like that!!!

I really...

Come on, Happy!! Plue!! We're going!!!

AGHAA!!

PU-PUII!!

カ カ STMP

カ カ STMP

カ カ STMP

SLAM

Puuun?

And I can't get Lucy involved in this!

What the heck am I doing?

I can't get caught up in emotions...

I don't have...

The next day at Fairy Tail...

I wonder if Gray is all right?

They got injured in a pillow fight right after finishing a job.

How can anybody get that badly injured in a pillow fight?

What is that?

Lucy!!! I was the winner, right?!!

Huh?! You're the one who lost!!!

But even so, you lost!!!

I don't care what it is, I give my all!!!

First of all, why do you have to get all worked up over a pillow fight?

Are there winners and losers in a pillow fight?

Cut the racket!

HUMPH

Lucy's not half bad!

Ohh!! I've never seen anybody besides Erza stop those two!!

W-We deeply apologize.

No!! Do I look like that shallow a person?!

Are you still mad at my little practical joke?

You think so? I think I'm acting like I always do.

Lucy... You've been in a bad mood for a while.

I can help.

No... Thank you anyway.

Sorry... It's just that I've had a lot to think over.

Loke!! Where are you?!!

I could ask you the same thing!!

Who do all of you think you are?!

I think Loke is just awful!

Where's Loke?

CHATTER

CHATTER

CHATTER

CHATTER

Say, is Loke here?

He even did it with me!!

Me too!!!

Arrg!! I hate to say it, but he did the same with me!!!

Last night, he suddenly hits me with a break-up speech!!

They all consider themselves to be Loke's girlfriend.

The girls of the town.

What is this?

I doubt it...

It couldn't be that he's found somebody else, could it?!!

J-Just calm down...

Why would he suddenly say something like that?!!

Who is it?!! Is it someone in this guild?!!

Honestly!!! Don't involve me in situations like this, Mira-san!!!

TMP
TMP
TMP

And that chest...

She could be considered cute by some...

Who is that woman?!!

She couldn't be Loke's other woman, could she...?

ZIIIING!!

キュ ズ-ズ-
ズ-

Lucy!! Save me!!

Wait a—

And that's what happened, Old Master Cru.

Hmaa...

Celestial Spirit
Southern Cross
Constellation Crux

AKA: Old Master Cru

FWAA

ふわ

ふわ

FWAA

Hmaa...

But I somehow get the feeling that he wasn't actually joking.

I just suddenly got all angry...

...then I just gave up and went home.

Hmaa
...

I was hoping that you could help me find out what was between Loke and that celestial spirit wizard in his past.

FWAA
ふわ

FWAA

ふ

Don't worry. He's searching his memory.

No he isn't!!! He's definitely sleeping !!!

He's just sleeping, Lucy!!!!

ZZZZZ

ZZZ

ZZZZZ

He would know which celestial wizard called which spirit through what gate and at what point in the past.

ZZZZZ

Old Master Cru is a specialist in celestial spirit lore.

He knows all that has ever passed through the gates between the celestial world and the human world.

DIAAAHH!!!!

Personal information is protected even in the celestial world, so I cannot be too specific.

HMAA

Cru, have you remembered something?

However, the celestial wizard with whom Loke had a relationship...

...went by the name of Karen Lilica.

Karen Lilica?!!!

She was a real beauty, and even made the gatefold of *Sorcerer* magazine!!

She's a really famous celestial wizard!!

You know of her, Lucy?

She was a guild wizard?

But she passed away a few years ago on a job.

Yeah...I'm pretty sure she was a member of Blue Pegasus.

Hmaa :

I cannot say any more on that subject.

Wait a minute !!

So tell me... What was Karen and Loke's relationship?

Huh ?!!!

No. This time, he's sleeping.

Ah!! So he says, but he went back to searching his memory!!

ZZZZZZ

"...much longer to live!!"

"I don't have..."

Karen and Loke...

What?

SVAAA

Aaah!!!

Lucy, you'd better come quick!!!

What is it, Lucy?

What is this bad premonition of mine...?

What?!

Loke left Fairy Tail!!!!

I was thinking that he's been acting a little strange lately.

I don't know!! Everybody's looking for him!!!

Wh-Why?!

ZLIP

Hey!! Lucy!!! Where are you thinking of looking?!!

TMP
TMP
TMP
TMP

WHOOSH

It couldn't be that...

EART

!

SHK

Lucy !!!

Every-body's searching for you.

SHK

SHK

Celestial Wizard Karen.

Your owner.

That's Karen's grave, right? Over there.

So you realized that I was a celestial spirit, huh?

. . . .

So I finally arrived at the truth about you.

After all, I am a celestial wizard, and I've made contracts with quite a few spirits myself.

Contract

Normally whenever an owner of a key dies, the contract with the spirit is null and void.

And the spirit is forced back into the celestial world until a new key owner arrives.

Con | tract

Free

To the next owner.

But I should have figured it out sooner.

SHK

SHK

143

There must have been some reason for you not to return to the celestial world.

With Karen dead, your contract should have been broken, but you remained in the human world.

Being in the wrong world drains your life force...

...and eventually it ends in death.

Humans cannot live in the celestial world.

And celestial spirits can't live in the human world.

Yes... But I've reached my limit.

My power just won't come out anymore.

Three years?!! One year should have been impossible!!

It's been three years.

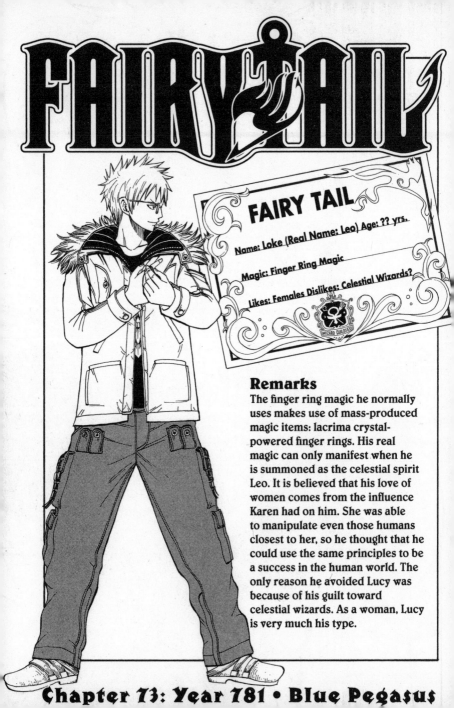

FAIRY TAIL

FAIRY TAIL

Name: Loke (Real Name: Leo) Age: ?? yrs.

Magic: Finger Ring Magic

Likes: Females Dislikes: Celestial Wizards?

Remarks
The finger ring magic he normally
uses makes use of mass-produced
magic items: lacrima crystal-
powered finger rings. His real
magic can only manifest when he
is summoned as the celestial spirit
Leo. It is believed that his love of
women comes from the influence
Karen had on him. She was able
to manipulate even those humans
closest to her, so he thought that he
could use the same principles to be
a success in the human world. The
only reason he avoided Lucy was
because of his guilt toward
celestial wizards. As a woman, Lucy
is very much his type.

Chapter 73: Year 781 • Blue Pegasus

SHH

SHHHHHH

You killed Karen...

SHHHH

...You killed your owner...?

SHH

FWAAA

But...

I will remain like this and vanish.

A spirit who kills his owner can't return to the celestial world.

SHH

SHHHHHH

It seems I've become used to the human world...

And after three months...

It's been three months. I think it's about time I made peace with Karen.

I can't seem to stop the drain on my life force, but it isn't nearly as hard on me as before...

If she abuses Aries again, I can always come back to help.

It wasn't very long after that when I heard the rumors in town of Karen's death.

Apparently she died on a job.

HAHH

HAHH

She went on a job in that condition and lost her life...

It was my fault that Karen couldn't summon any other celestial spirits.

HAHH

HAHH

It's the same as if I had murdered her myself.

Wait!! Hang in there!!!

And because of the events of that day, I was made unable to return to the celestial world.

SSSS

All celestial spirits who disobey their masters' orders are rejected by the celestial world.

166

Chapter 74: Celestial Spirit King

Her death was just an accident, right?!!!

That's not the same as actually murdering Karen!!!

But this isn't right !!!

Open !!!! Gate of the Lion Palace !!!!

Take Loke back to the celestial world!!!!

だーん!

GWMM

Lucy
...

Open !!!

Please !!!!

It isn't enough !!!

VSSH

You've done enough...

Please stop...

How can anybody watch a friend vanish before their eyes and not try to do something ?!!!

Lucy!!! You can't use up all your power at once like that!!!!

Nnngg!!!

It won't open!!! A celestial spirit in a contract with a human can't defy her and ever hope to return!!!!

I'll show you that I can do a forced opening of the gate to the celestial world!!!

I promised you, didn't I?!! I'm going to save you!!!

You'll wind up disappearing with me if you don't stop!!!!

Stop it!!! You're starting to assimilate into the celestial world!!!!

174

"King"...?!! You mean the top celestial spirit?!!

Wh-What's he doing here?!!

Old friend... Thou hast broken covenant with mankind and murdered thy key holder!!!

Thy act was indirect. However through that inaction, the same result did come to pass.

Thou hast been denied return to the celestial world.

Old Friend...

...this law alone I cannot change!

S-Stop it, Lucy!!!

Wait a minute!! That's not fair!!!

He's been tortured for three years!!!

That can't be!!! He can't have appeared here just because Lucy said she'd change the rule!!!

A tiny event like that, and the king himself...

TREMBLE

TREMBLE

It pains my heart to hear my old friend's plea, but...

And he did it for friendship!!! He had to do it for Aries's sake!!!!

. . . . .

Uhn...

Quit trying to do the impossible!!!!

It may have been only for a moment, but you could've died doing that!!!!

!

...perhaps the fault lies with the law.

If you will speak thus unto my old friend...

Leo committed a crime for the sake of his fellow spirit, Aries.

Now his old friend attempts to save his life.

Leo...Thy return to the celestial world has thus been granted.

In recognition of these beautiful bonds of loyalty...

...this case shall be judged as *an exception.*

GRIN

You know, you're pretty cool for a bearded old fart!

Wait, just a second...

I...

WHOOSH

You are pardoned. Give your thanks unto the paths of the stars!

If thou yet wish to receive punishment for thy crime...

...then we sentence thee to live at the service of thy friend and lend her thy aid.

That your life should be devoted to protecting her.

For that is the value of thy friend.

ZPOOSH

...... You heard him!

TO BE CONTINUED

AFTERWORD

Man, am I busy!! Yeah, for a manga-ka that's a great thing to be able to say, but I'm way too busy!! If you want to know why, it's because I have another manga series—this time a monthly series. I've done this in the past, doing a monthly and a weekly series at the same time, but this time there are so many more pages required than last time! So the pace is so much different than before. By the way, when I was only doing a weekly manga, the amount of work equaled twenty pages of manga, twenty pages of *name* (the Japanese term for a rough-sketched story and dialogue), plus a couple of color pieces and small odd jobs. But the quantity of work I had last week was forty-three manga pages, sixty-nine pages of *name,* four color pages, and tons of those small, odd jobs. What the heck was that week all about?!! The only thing I can do is laugh about it!! Yeah, it was an unusually heavy week that included a short story, so the page numbers were artificially high, but even so, my regular work week is about twice as busy as before. Man! It's unbelievable!!

Recently I met another creator, and was asked what my motivation is for doing all of that work. I don't know how to answer that question. I never even considered the concept of motivation. Of course, I love manga, and that's why I draw it. But that's the basic assumption for any manga-ka. In my case, maybe it includes journeyman-style training. That probably sums it up. I've been doing this work for over ten years, but I can't seem to get good at drawing. (Ha ha!) Is it true that if I draw a lot, I'll become better? Normally, you'd think so…Anyway, I'm busy! Really busy! And that's what comes out of my mouth when I'm talking to the people around me, but inside I'm having so much fun, I can hardly contain it! I can draw a whole lot of manga! My manga will be read by a whole lot of people! That's probably my motivation, huh?

: By the way, I entered six years ago, bringing Elfman and Lisanna with me.

Erza: Natsu entered seven years ago, and Gray had entered even before I did.

Lucy: Huh? You guys have been in the guild a long time! It hasn't even been a year for me!

Erza: The story of my life before Fairy Tail is touched on in Volume 10.

Mira: I'm interested in learning about that!

 : What was that? You just casually throw a preview of the next volume into the conversation?

Mira: Okay, the final question.

Who is the heroine of Fairy Tail? Lucy or Erza?

 : *!!!*

Mira: Nobody cares who the "heroine" is, right?

Lucy: What do you mean "nobody?!" I mean, people would automatically assume it's me, right?

 : Well...I feel a little embarrassed being addressed as the heroine, but...Am I truly being looked upon in that fashion?

Lucy: Wait a minute!! What are you blushing for?!!

Mira: Certainly at first glance, one would think it's Lucy, but I hear that Erza has more fans.

 : *You're kidding!!!*

Erza: Is that so?

Lucy: Wait!! Just look at the cover of Volume 9! It's me!! All me!! I carry the entire cover all by myself!!

Mira: If you look closely, you see an awful lot of celestial spirits there too.

Erza: Lucy, did you know? They included a poster of me in *Weekly Magazine*.

Lucy: Waaaaaah!!

Erza: And that was only me. Heh heh...

Lucy: Waaaaaaaaaahh!

Mira: Well, none of this bickering will settle the matter. So why don't we ask the author directly?

------- *And so...* -------

Mashima: You're asking who the heroine is?

Lucy: It's me, right?! You love drawing pictures of me, don't you?!!

Erza: Do not forget that you drew a poster that was me and me alone.

Mashima: I give up. I think it's okay for the readers to decide who they think the heroine is for themselves.

Mira: Exactly! Nobody cares who it is! ♥

Mashima: Frankly, I think it's okay for the heroine to be Tomeko from Tokekko Restaurant.

 : *It is not okay!!*

Special Request

Explain the Mysteries...

... of Fairy Tail

From the Counter at Fairy Tail...

 : All you readers out there, hello! ♥

 : Hello! You're in a good mood today, Lucy!

Lucy: Sure! It's the ninth volume, and the stories were all about me!! It's like Volume 9 was drawn especially for me! ♥

Mira: That's what it means to be a heroine, I guess, huh? Well, while you're in such a good mood, let's get started on the questions.

How many sets of armor total can Erza requip into?

Lucy: That question is pretty painful...er...I mean sharp!

Mira: The two of us can't answer it, so let's call in the woman herself. Introducing our special guest, Erza!

 : Mm.

Lucy: Don't just say, "Mm"! If you don't come up with some greeting, you'll lose popularity points!

Erza: No...Well...I suppose I am not used to this...Uh...Hello.

Mira: So about the question we just heard. Erza, how many suits of armor do you have?

Erza: Many.

 : Wait a second! None of the readers will really count that as an answer! You're going to have to do better than that to increase your point score!

Mira: What are popularity points exactly?

Erza: I have more than a hundred different types. I haven't counted them all myself, but I also count within their ranks dresses and kimono.

Lucy: Requipping is such a great concept! Dressing must be a breeze!

Mira: On to the next question.

I am Erza. Nice to meet you.

How long has Erza been in the Fairy Tail guild?

 : Eight years. That brings back memories.

Continued on the

The Fairy Tail Guild d'Art is an explosion of fan art! Please send in your black-and-white art on large postcard stock!! Those chosen to be published will get a signed mini poster! ♪ Make sure you write your real name and address on the back of your postcard!

d'ART

◀ Just a little while ago I drew a side story like that. An Erza in a school uniform, huh?

Gunma Prefecture, Kayo

◀ This one's very cute!! And well done!

Iwate Prefecture, K5 Minamikaze

◀ Whoa! This one has some great artistic sense!

Iwate Prefecture, Sena Minazuki

◀ It seems that the battle between these two has gotten itself a good reputation.

Hyōgo Prefecture, Kōsuke Shimoda

◀ A fan from my previous work. I'm so happy I could cry!

Hokkaido, Seiryu Tanaka

Alzack Connel

◀ Are you a part of the Gloomy Character Fan Club? Maybe now, huh?

A cool guy! ✦

Aichi Prefecture, Chibō

◀ Whoa! Galeel's scary! This is one page that's got him pinned!

Niigata Prefecture, Tomohiko Enamoto

◀ Thank you!! Keep on rooting for me, please!
I love everybody!! Fairy Tail's the best!!!

Chiba Prefecture, Koharu

◀ And there's Tomeko!!! One came!!! Yeah, but actually there are about twenty other pictures of her! (Ha ha!)

Ishikawa Prefecture, Natsu vs. Haru

Send to Hiro Mashima, Kodansha Comics
451 Park Ave. South, 7th Floor, New York, NY 10016

GUILD

By sending in letters or postcards you give us permission to give your name, address, postal code and any other information you include to the author as is. Please keep that in mind.

Rejection Corner

I don't want to be rejected! ♥

Saitama Prefecture, Keisuke Gōtō

▲ You can't get everything you want!

Baliko

Shizuoka Prefecture, Junichi Iwahori

▶ Ehh? By the way, it's Baigo. Although Baliko makes a nice girl's name.

Miyazaki Prefecture, Sayuri

▶ A-Another rare character. We only saw it on a splash page once...

Ibaragi Prefecture, Masahiro Ishizaki

▶ I wonder when his next active appearance will be...?

FAIRY TAIL
Happy New Year!

Miyagi Prefecture, Shion

▶ Happy New Year's to you! And thanks for all of the New Year's cards!

FAIRY TAIL

Shizuoka Prefecture, Kahori Mat-sushima

▶ Wow, that's cute! Is she doing cosplay as a fairy?

Weekly SORCERER
Nice to see you!

Hyōgo Prefecture, Puririn

▶ These appeared in a limited edition publication. Actually they're based on editors of mine.

About the Creator

HIRO MASHIMA was born May 3, 1977, in the Nagano prefecture. His series *Rave Master* has made him one of the most popular manga artists in America. *Fairy Tail*, currently being serialized in *Weekly Shōnen Magazine*, is his latest creation.

Translation Notes

Japanese is a tricky language for most Westerners, and translation is often more art than science. For your edification and reading pleasure, here are notes on some of the places where we could have gone in a different direction in our translation of the work, or where a Japanese cultural reference is used.

General Notes:
Wizard

In the original Japanese version of *Fairy Tail*, you'll find panels in which the English word "wizard" is part of the original illustration. So this translation has taken that as its inspiration and translated the word *madôshi* as "wizard." But *madôshi's* meaning is similar to certain Japanese words that have been borrowed by the English language, such as judo (the soft way) and kendo (the way of the sword). *Madô* is the way of magic, and *madôshi* are those who follow the way of magic. So although the word "wizard" is used in the original dialogue, a Japanese reader would be likely to think not of traditional Western wizards such as Merlin or Gandalf, but of martial artists.

Names

Hiro Mashima has graciously agreed to provide official English spellings for just about all of the characters in *Fairy Tail*. Because this version of *Fairy Tail* is the first publication of most of these spellings, there will inevitably be differences between these spellings and some of the fan interpretations that may have spread throughout the Web or in other fan circles. Rest assured that the spellings contained in this book are the spellings that Mashima-sensei wanted for *Fairy Tail*.

Bento, page 34

The traditional boxed lunch of Japan usually features a main course on a bed of rice and includes pickled veggies, salad, cooked egg, and other foods along with sweet beans for dessert. Women are known for waking up early and fixing elaborate bento boxes. Single girls prepare them for themselves or their boyfriends, while mothers fix bento boxes for their children's school lunches.

Feminist, page 36

In America, the word "feminist" has taken on nuances of a radical activist for women's rights. In Japan, the connotations are much broader, spanning the range from activist to someone who simply likes women.

Passionate Fish, page 45

The title of the top book the librarian is holding was written in Japanese, *Jōnetsu-gyo*, which means "Passionate Fish" or "Passion Fish." One might assume that, as translator, I would use the name of the movie, *Passion Fish*, for the translation, but it did not seem appropriate in this instance. When the movie came out, the Japanese title was not in Japanese, but instead used the English words in Japanese *katakana* characters, *Passhon Fisshu*. Since Mashima-sensei didn't use the proper name for the movie title, it seemed wrong for the translation to use the proper title of the movie either.

Mabô and Yanbô, page 66

There are many types of nicknames in Japanese, and this is one
example. One takes the first syllable of the name and adds *bô* to the end
(or *nbô* depending on phonics and the whim of the one assigning the
nickname). This is generally a nickname used by men for male friends,
and although it is still heard now and again, the popularity of that
nickname declined decades ago. The use of the nicknames indicate that
Master Makarov and Yajima are either old, very close friends, or former
classmates.

Ramen, *chashu* pork, page 66

The Chinese barbecue pork, *char siu*, is pronounced *chashu* in Japan, and
the most common dish associated with *chashu* is ramen. One can order
chashu Ramen as a menu item in most ramen restaurants/Chinese
restaurants in Japan, or one can order extra *chashu* to be added
to other ramen dishes such as Miso Ramen. *Chashu* consists of thin
slices of pork (usually pork shoulder), and one usually only receives two
or three slices per ramen dish.

Ebb and Sea Bream, page 119

There is a phrase in Japanese, *isshin-ittai*, which means "ebb and flow." Of course it refers to the tides, but it also indicates the ups and downs of one's life. But in Japanese pun-loving fashion, here the normal *kanji* for *tai* has been replaced with a different *kanji*, also pronounced *tai*, but meaning "sea bream." Not the easiest pun to try to translate, but since English has few uses for the word "ebb" in any other context than "ebb and flow," juxtaposing "ebb and " with "sea bream" gives one the idea that someone is trying to make a joke—no matter how less-than-hilarious the pun was in this English translation.

Hmaa, page 133

This is simply one of those mumbling vocalizations that old men make in between sentences and phrases. I left the sound the same as in the Japanese.

Memphis Ring, page 150

The Memphis Ring is a magic item that can be found in the Japanese massively multi-player role-playing game (MMRPG), Strugarden Neo. The item is a finger ring with enough power to defeat a boss in the game.

Old Friend, page 178

In Japanese, the celestial spirit king used the term *furuki tomo*, which is a rather archaic way of saying "old friend." I was unable to find any other instances where this phrase was used in Japanese history or literature, so I can't claim to be an expert in the nuances of this phrase. Only that he used it as a way of saying "you" in the Japanese—even to Lucy who he had just met. The rest of his speech was rather archaic as well, and so the translation used "thees," "thous," and similar language to convey that concept.

Photo of the Mashima Group and
Yoshikawa Group combined.

I've been hanging out with Miki
Yoshikawa-sensei (I usually follow
her name with "-chan" but...) for
more than five years. She has been
a good friend at times, and at other
times a good rival. Although she
started in manga after me, she's a
well-respected member of my circle
of friends. Since we're both so
busy, we are only able to hang out
together once or twice a year, but
during the times we can get both
of our groups together, it's really
fun! On the day of this picture, we
were playing video games from the
morning on....What a great group
of adults, huh? Ah ha ha ha!! They
were really fun people!

—Hiro Mashima

Honorifics Explained

Throughout the Kodansha Comics books, you will find Japanese honorifics left intact in the translations. For those not familiar with how the Japanese use honorifics and, more important, how they differ from American honorifics, we present this brief overview.

Politeness has always been a critical facet of Japanese culture. Ever since the feudal era, when Japan was a highly stratified society, use of honorifics—which can be defined as polite speech that indicates relationship or status—has played an essential role in the Japanese language. When addressing someone in Japanese, an honorific usually takes the form of a suffix attached to one's name (example: "Asuna-san"), is used as a title at the end of one's name, or appears in place of the name itself (example: "Negi-sensei," or simply "Sensei").

Honorifics can be expressions of respect or endearment. In the context of manga and anime, honorifics give insight into the nature of the relationship between characters. Many English translations leave out these important honorifics and therefore distort the feel of the original Japanese. Because Japanese honorifics contain nuances that English honorifics lack, it is our policy at Kodansha not to translate them. Here, instead, is a guide to some of the honorifics you may encounter in Kodansha Comics.

-**san**: This is the most common honorific and is equivalent to Mr., Miss, Ms., or Mrs. It is the all-purpose honorific and can be used in any situation where politeness is required.

-**sama**: This is one level higher than "-san" and is used to confer great respect.

-**dono**: This comes from the word "tono," which means "lord." It is an even higher level than "-sama" and confers utmost respect.

-kun: This suffix is used at the end of boys' names to express familiarity or endearment. It is also sometimes used by men among friends, or when addressing someone younger or of a lower station.

-chan: This is used to express endearment, mostly toward girls. It is also used for little boys, pets, and even between lovers. It gives a sense of childish cuteness.

Bozu: This is an informal way to refer to a boy, similar to the English terms "kid" and "squirt."

Sempai/
Senpai: This title suggests that the addressee is one's senior in a group or organization. It is most often used in a school setting, where underclassmen refer to their upperclassmen as "sempai." It can also be used in the workplace, such as when a newer employee addresses an employee who has seniority in the company.

Kohai: This is the opposite of "sempai" and is used toward underclassmen in school or newcomers in the workplace. It connotes that the addressee is of a lower station.

Sensei: Literally meaning "one who has come before," this title is used for teachers, doctors, or masters of any profession or art.

-[blank]: This is usually forgotten in these lists, but it is perhaps the most significant difference between Japanese and English. The lack of honorific means that the speaker has permission to address the person in a very intimate way. Usually, only family, spouses, or very close friends have this kind of permission. Known as *yobisute*, it can be gratifying when someone who has earned the intimacy starts to call one by one's name without an honorific. But when that intimacy hasn't been earned, it can be very insulting.

Preview of Volume 10

We're pleased to present you with a preview from volume 10, now available from Kodansha Comics. Check out our Web site (www.kodanshacomics.com) for more details!

!!?

You're a celestial spirit? **!!!**

Neither is Virgo. You know her. She looks just like a regular girl, right?

Hold it a second! You aren't a cow or a horse or anything!

I never even guessed.

Well, I guess it boils down to that.

STARE

STARE

STARE

STARE

Lion? **!!!**

Loke is from the Lion Palace.

Now that you mention it, I guess you're right.

Nope! She can also look like a huge gorilla!

Hey, that's cool!

Come to think of it, you still look exactly the same. There's no problem with that?

Lion... Isn't that like a grown-up cat?

Exactly.

Exactly wrong!!!

I have to be Lucy's knight in shining armor, appearing to rescue her whenever she's in danger.

It might not be possible from now on. Lucy is my owner now, and I'm at her bidding.

Must be nice, huh? I want a celestial spirit of my own!

Huh? What kind of spirit?

Hey! Put me down!!

And thus, we head off to discuss our future in depth.

You can go home now.

Absolutely true! Celestial spirits are meant for love!

Celestial wizards don't use their spirits as punching bags or sparring partners!!

Here I am, knowing everything a guy needs to know to be a dragon slayer! But what's the point if I don't have a dragon to fight with?!

A dragon!! What else?!!

PWIK

SHH SHH SHH SHH

Here!

FLIP

Wait just a minute!

SHH SHH

I can't spend long amounts of time in the human world anymore...

What are these?

These are tickets to a resort hotel I intended to go to with my girlfriends, but now...

A Kodansha Comics trade Paperback Original

Fairy Tail volume 9 copyright © 2008 Hiro Mashima
English translation copyright © 2009 Hiro Mashima

Published in the United States by Kodansha Comics, an imprint of Kodansha USA Publishing, LLC., New York.

Publication rights for this English edition arranged through Kodansha Ltd., Tokyo.

First published in Japan in 2008 by Kodansha Ltd., Tokyo

ISBN 978-1-612-62280-4

Printed in the United States of America

www.kodanshacomics.com

9   8   7   6

Translator/Adapter—William Flanagan
Lettering—North Market Street Graphics

TOMARE!

[STOP!]

You're going the wrong way!

Manga is a completely different type of reading experience.

To start at the *beginning*, go to the *end*!

That's right! Authentic manga is read the traditional Japanese way—from right to left, exactly the opposite of how American books are read. It's easy to follow: Just go to the other end of the book and read each page—and each panel—from right side to left side, starting at the top right. Now you're experiencing manga as it was meant to be!